STUDY GUIDE

The Attributes of God

Steven J. Lawson

LIGONIER.ORG | 800-435-4343

Copyright © 2013 Ligonier Ministries
421 Ligonier Court, Sanford, FL 32771
E-mail: info@ligonier.org
All rights reserved.
No reproduction of this work without permission.
Printed in the United States of America.

1

Introduction to the Attributes of God

MESSAGE INTRODUCTION

Worthwhile relationships are based on knowledge. When we meet someone for the first time, we do not consider that we really know that person until we have the opportunity to learn more about that person, such as his or her history, personality, likes, dislikes, and desires. As we come to know more about a new acquaintance, we better understand how to carry on a relationship with that person. In the same way, a vibrant relationship with the triune God must be rooted in a firm understanding of who He reveals Himself to be in His Word. In this message, Dr. Steven J. Lawson presents an overview of God's defining attributes and invites us to pursue a more intimate and worshipful relationship with Him.

SCRIPTURE READINGS

Exodus 15:11–13; Psalm 55:8–9; Psalm 89:5–8

TEACHING OBJECTIVES

1. To provide definitions and examples of divine attributes
2. To discuss the ways in which these attributes describe the triune God
3. To show how theology affects life and worship

QUOTATIONS

It is evident that man never attains to a true self-knowledge until he has previously contemplated the face of God, and come down after such contemplation to look into himself.

—John Calvin

This is eternal life, that we may know the Father and his Son Jesus Christ, whom he has sent, in the power and by the grace of the Holy Spirit. In his presence is life and joy forevermore, not simply for us, but for others beyond, for those yet to believe and for those not yet born, for generations to come and beyond that for eternity.

—Robert Letham

LECTURE OUTLINE

A. The Importance of a Right Understanding of God
   1. It has been said that what comes into a person's mind when he or she thinks about God is the most important thing about him or her.
      a. High views of God lead to high and holy living, worship, evangelism, and service.
      b. Low views of God lead to a low and base way of interacting with God, self, and others.
   2. This teaching series will seek to promote a high view of God by examining fifteen of God's attributes.
      a. By gaining an accurate understanding of who God is, Christians become better equipped to understand themselves and the world around them.
      b. Because every area of one's life and worldview is influenced by one's understanding of God, it is essential to understand His defining attributes.
   3. An *attribute* refers to a quality or characteristic that belongs to a person.
      a. God's attributes define and describe who God is.
      b. Although we cannot understand the full depth of God's character, this teaching series will explore some of the main characteristics of God that are mentioned in Scripture.

B. God's Distinct Attributes: An Overview
   1. God is *self-existent* (*a se*): He has life in Himself and depends on no one.
   2. God is *spiritual*: He does not have a material body and is transcendent.
   3. God is *sovereign*: He rules over all things with absolute control.
   4. God is *holy*: He is pure, blameless, and flawless in all of His being.
   5. God is *omnipresent*: He is boundless, present in all places at once.
   6. God is *omniscient*: He knows all things.
   7. God is *omnipotent*: He is all-powerful.
   8. God is *immutable*: He never changes.
   9. God is *truthful*: He speaks accurately and authoritatively.
   10. God is *wise*: He enacts His perfect will by the highest ends and means.
   11. God is *good*: He deals bounteously with His creatures.
   12. God is *gracious*: He freely bestows salvation on undeserving sinners.
   13. God is *loving*: He demonstrates selfless love for His children.
   14. God is *foreknowing*: He has known and loved His people from eternity.
   15. God is *righteous in wrath*: He loves purity and punishes impurity.

C. Divine Attributes in Proper Perspective
1. Some of God's attributes are called "incommunicable attributes," and others are called "communicable attributes."
   a. God's incommunicable attributes, such as immutability and omniscience, belong to Him alone.
   b. God's communicable attributes, such as love and wisdom, find their fullest expression in Him but can also be displayed on a smaller scale by His human image-bearers.
2. God's attributes are not independent of one another but are interconnected.
   a. These divine attributes are present in the entire Godhead; they are possessed by all three persons of the Trinity.
   b. Each of these attributes has always belonged to God and will always belong to Him.
      i. God neither gains nor loses attributes.
      ii. Those who claim that God is different in the Old and New Testaments misunderstand the nature of divine attributes.
   c. Each attribute characterizes every other attribute.
      i. Complex beings have separate, identifiable parts, but simple beings do not.
      ii. Because God is a simple being, it is impossible to divide Him into parts, so as to separate His goodness from His wisdom or His wrath.
      iii. Instead, each attribute describes the others; for example, God's holiness is immutable, omnipotent, and eternal.
3. God's attributes have crucial implications for our day-to-day lives.
   a. This is not a purely academic or intellectual subject.
   b. Rather, an accurate understanding of God is foundational if we desire to know Him, serve Him, and become like Him.
   c. Only when we know God can we truly worship Him.
   d. Knowledge of God keeps us anchored as we minister in His name and proclaim His truth to others.

STUDY QUESTIONS

1. The attribute that best describes God's kind and generous dealings with believers, unbelievers, and inanimate creation is His _____.
   a. Goodness
   b. Omnipotence
   c. Grace
   d. Sovereignty

2. Some of God's attributes apply exclusively to the Father, while others mainly describe the Son or the Spirit.
   a. True
   b. False

3. God's communicable attributes are His qualities which _____.
   a. Can only belong to God
   b. Are unknowable apart from special revelation
   c. Are most easy to describe to others
   d. God demonstrates perfectly but humans can share imperfectly

4. Each of God's attributes is _____.
   a. A separate part of God
   b. Unrelated to the others
   c. Eternally part of God's character
   d. Only found in the Godhead

5. God is better described as a simple being, rather than as a complex being.
   a. True
   b. False

BIBLE STUDY AND DISCUSSION QUESTIONS

1. Why is a person's belief in God important? In what ways do these beliefs shape other areas of a person's life?

2. How does a biblical understanding of God's attributes impact the way that you perceive yourself and other people?

3. As Dr. Lawson observes, our theology determines our doxology. Consider some of the different approaches to worship that you have seen in churches today; what are the different views of God that undergird these views of worship?

4. Of the attributes of God mentioned in this message, which one is the most familiar to you? Which of these are you most curious to learn about?

2

The Aseity of God

MESSAGE INTRODUCTION

Of God's many distinct attributes, one of the most difficult for finite human beings to come to terms with is His aseity, or self-existence. Unlike us, God has neither beginning nor end, and He is not dependent upon anyone or anything. In this message, as we consider God's limitless abundance and our own neediness, Dr. Lawson invites us to seek full satisfaction and delight in the one who is the limitless source of all things.

SCRIPTURE READINGS

Psalm 90:1–4; Romans 11:33–36; 1 Corinthians 8:5–6; Revelation 4:8

TEACHING OBJECTIVES

1. To discuss the implications of God's eternal and self-sustaining nature
2. To recognize our inability to comprehend God's boundless character
3. To invite Christians to take refuge in the all-sufficiency of God

QUOTATIONS

There is something exceedingly improving to the mind in a contemplation of the Divinity. It is a subject so vast, that all our thoughts are lost in its immensity; so deep, that our pride is drowned in its infinity. Other subjects we can compass and grapple with; in them we feel a kind of self-content, and go our way with the thought, "Behold I am wise." But when we come to this master-science, finding that our plumb-line cannot sound its depth, and that our eagle eye cannot see its height, we turn away . . . with the solemn exclamation, "I am but of yesterday, and know nothing."

—Charles Spurgeon

God was under no constraint, no obligation, no necessity to create. That He chose to do so was purely a sovereign act on His part caused by nothing outside of Himself, determined by nothing but His own mere good pleasure.

—A.W. Pink

LECTURE OUTLINE

A. God of Limitless Majesty
   1. One of the attributes that most distinguishes God from humanity is His aseity.
      a. The word *aseity* comes from Latin roots meaning "from" and "self."
      b. God's aseity refers to His eternal self-existence.
   2. God has always been in existence.
      a. In the beginning, God was already present (Gen. 1:1).
      b. God's rule over the cosmos is everlasting (Ps. 93:2).
   3. Unlike human beings, God does not have a time or place of origin.

B. The Source of All Things
   1. The finite universe owes its existence to the infinite God.
   2. Before the creation of time and space, the triune God existed eternally without anything or anyone else in the universe.
      a. Though alone, God was not lonely.
      b. The three persons of the Trinity enjoyed perfect satisfaction, fellowship, and delight in one another.
   3. God created the universe not by necessity but for His own glory.
      a. God did not lack anything when He was alone, and He was not under any constraint or obligation to bring anything else into existence.
      b. God's act of creation therefore displays His love and majesty.
   4. God is the source of all life.
      a. Because He is completely self-existent, He is not caused by or dependent upon anything outside Himself (John 5:26).
      b. As His creatures, our physical life, spiritual life, and even eternal life with Him all have God as their source (Acts 17:28).
   5. All things are "from him and through him and to him" (Rom. 11:36).
      a. That all things are "from" God expresses that He is the source of all things.
      b. That all things are "through" God expresses that He is the means of all things.
      c. That all things are "to" God expresses that He is the goal of all things.

C. Finite Children of an Infinite Father
   1. Because God is our source, we are made to live in fellowship with Him.
      a. As Augustine articulated, our hearts are restless until they find rest in God.

b. The greater our understanding of who God is, the more our own hearts become filled with contentment and satisfaction in Him.
2. Though we are insignificant compared to God, He invites us to bring all of our concerns to Him and trust Him with everything.
   a. We often wonder whether He cares about the small things in our lives or whether He is only concerned with the big things.
   b. However, compared to His greatness and self-sufficiency, all things in our lives are small; yet, He invites us to come to Him anyway.
3. Because God is all-sufficient, we can know that there is not a need in our lives that He cannot supply.

STUDY QUESTIONS

1. Scripture indicates that, before the creation of the universe, God's existence was characterized by _____.
   a. Loneliness
   b. Satisfaction
   c. Angelic praise
   d. Boredom

2. All human life, even the Christian's future immortality, depends on God as its source.
   a. True
   b. False

3. The fact that God is not caused by or dependent upon anything outside of Himself is primarily an illustration of His _____.
   a. Immutability
   b. Omnipotence
   c. Self-existence
   d. Transcendence

4. The statement in Romans 11:36 that all things are "through" God chiefly communicates the idea that He is the _____ of all things.
   a. Goal
   b. Overseer
   c. Source
   d. Means

5. Because God is limitless and boundless, it is best to bring only the big things in our lives to His attention.
   a. True
   b. False

BIBLE STUDY AND DISCUSSION QUESTIONS

1. Imagine that later today an unchurched friend asks you what you are learning in this study. How would you explain God's eternal and self-existent nature to that person?

2. Explain the statement "If anything exists, then something has always existed." What does this mean, and why is this important?

3. Did God need to create anything? Why did He bring the universe into existence?

4. Do you struggle with whether or not to bring "big" and "little" matters to God? How can a biblical understanding of God's aseity shape the way we present our needs and desires to God?

3

The Spirituality of God

MESSAGE INTRODUCTION

The concept of spirituality is used to communicate a variety of different ideas. For some, this word indicates a conscious commitment to the things of God. To others, to say that someone is spiritual is to suggest that he or she has a generic interest in religious or supernatural matters. However, to speak of God's spirituality is actually to identify Him as a spirit—an immaterial, invisible, and infinite being that is fundamentally distinct from material, visible, and finite creatures. In this message, Dr. Lawson investigates what it means to affirm that God is a spiritual being and why this aspect of His character is crucial to our understanding of who He is.

SCRIPTURE READINGS

John 1:18; John 4:23–24; 1 Timothy 1:16–17

TEACHING OBJECTIVES

1. To explore what it means that God is immaterial, invisible, and infinite
2. To describe the connection between God's spirituality and His presence with His people
3. To commend God's infinite and mysterious nature as an invitation to greater worship

QUOTATIONS

God is a Spirit, and has not a body like men.

—Catechism for Young Children

[Handwritten note at top: If I lived my life w/ the understanding that God is present w/ me, my life + decisions would be more Christ-like/different.]

Everywhere in the Old and in the New Testament, God is represented as a spiritual Being, without form, invisible, whom no man hath seen or can see; dwelling in the light which no man approach unto, and full of glory; as not only the creator, and preserver, but as the governor of all things; as everywhere present, and everywhere imparting life, and securing order.

—Charles Hodge

[Handwritten note: immensity – refers to God not being confined by space/universe.]

LECTURE OUTLINE

[Handwritten note: omnipresent – refers to God being everywhere in the universe.]

A. The Immaterial God
1. God is spirit and therefore does not have a material body (John 4:24).
2. When Scripture attributes human anatomy to God, it does so figuratively.
   a. The Bible speaks of God's hands (Jer. 18:6), eyes (2 Chron. 16:9), arms (Isa. 53:1), and ears (Ps. 130:2).
   b. God sometimes describes Himself using human qualities in order to reveal Himself to us in ways that we can most easily understand.
3. Rather than being a limitation, God's absence of a physical body is part of what makes Him the divine Lord of all.
   a. Since He has no body, God is not subject to spatial constraints.
   b. As such, God can be present in all places at all times.
   c. It is precisely because God does not have a physical body that He is able to keep His promises to be with His people (Matt. 28:20; Heb. 13:5).
4. Because God is spirit, we can be assured that wherever we go and no matter how alone we may feel, God is with us still.

B. The Invisible God
1. Because God does not have a material body, He cannot be seen by human eyes.
   a. Though people sometimes claim to have seen God, the truth is that He is invisible (1 Tim. 1:17).
   b. The only physical manifestation of God in human form is Jesus Christ, the God-man (John 1:18; Col. 1:15).
2. While we cannot actually see God, we must know Him through His revelation to us.
   a. We can know about God by examining the world that He has made.
   b. We can know about God by reading what the Bible says about Him.
   c. We can know about God by entering into a relationship with Jesus Christ, who is God in human form (John 1:14).
3. Because God is invisible, Christians must live by faith, hoping for the day when we shall be in His physical presence and see Him face-to-face.

C. The Infinite God
1. As a spirit being, God has no ontological boundaries or limits.
   a. The fullness of His being permeates every part of time and space.
   b. God's greatness surpasses human understanding.

Bonna Seat

3—The Spirituality of God

2. The mystery of God ought to heighten our sense of worship.
   a. If it were possible for us to figure out God completely, we would not be drawn to worship Him.
   b. Because He is beyond human comprehension, He brings us to our knees in wonder and amazement.
   c. Since we can never know God completely, there is always room for us to grow and deepen in our relationship with Him.

STUDY QUESTIONS

1. To say that God is spirit is to say that _____.
   a. The physical is ontologically inferior to the spiritual
   b. God is more of an idea than a concrete reality
   c. *(circled)* He does not have a material body
   d. Human beings, as mortal creatures, cannot interact with God

2. Why does Scripture use human anatomy to describe God?
   a. To show us what God is *not* like
   b. To depict what God would look like if He appeared in human form
   c. To convey the idea that God's body is made of spirit, not flesh
   d. *(circled)* To reveal God's character in a way that we can easily understand

3. Because God does not have a body, He is subject to severe spatial constraints.
   a. True
   b. *(circled)* False

4. All of the following *except* _____ are reliable ways to learn about God.
   a. Entering into a personal relationship with Jesus Christ
   b. *(circled)* Talking with people who attest that God appeared to them
   c. Reading the Bible
   d. Studying the physical world

5. The fullness of God's being exists in every part of the universe.
   a. *(circled)* True
   b. False

BIBLE STUDY AND DISCUSSION QUESTIONS

1. Does God have a body? What is true as a result? *God does not have a physical body*
2. Though God is immaterial, Scripture affirms the original goodness of our human bodies and reminds us that we will live eternally in a resurrected and embodied state. What are ways that we can delight in and glorify God through our materiality and embodiment?
   We can worship Him
   We can follow Jesus Christ's teaching.

Hebrews 13 — I will never, never leave you or forsake you

3. In what way did understanding God's spirituality bring comfort to Dr. Lawson when he was a college student? How does this divine attribute address a situation in your life? *He is always w/ me.*

4. How will a better understanding of God affect your worship?

   It will allow us to better understand His awesomeness

   The more we understand the awesomeness of God, the more we value him.

4

The Sovereignty of God

MESSAGE INTRODUCTION

Resounding throughout the pages of Scripture is the proclamation that God is King. And the concept most closely associated with His kingship is His sovereignty. To say that God is sovereign is not to say merely that He is stronger than everyone else, although this is true. Rather, to call Him sovereign is to ascribe to Him a rule and authority that transcends space and time, leaving nothing outside its scope. In this lesson, Dr. Lawson examines the nature and extent of God's sovereign rule, showing how a biblical understanding of this topic can change the way we view the progress of history, the events of the present world, and the circumstances of our own lives.

SCRIPTURE READINGS

Psalm 33:1–22; Psalm 93:1–5; Ephesians 1:3–12

TEACHING OBJECTIVES

1. To explain the foundational importance of God's sovereignty
2. To demonstrate the extent of God's sovereignty, which stretches through space and time
3. To instill awe in the face of God's limitless power
4. To show how God's sovereignty ought to provide comfort to those facing adversity

QUOTATIONS

There is not a square inch in the whole domain of our human existence over which Christ, who is Sovereign over all, does not cry: "Mine!"
—Abraham Kuyper

God's sovereignty has ever appeared to me a great part of his glory. It has often been my delight to approach God, and adore him as a sovereign God.
—Jonathan Edwards

LECTURE OUTLINE

A. The God Who Reigns
   1. God's sovereignty refers to His right to rule, govern, and preside over all things.
      a. One who is sovereign is supreme in rank, power, and authority.
      b. The Scriptures repeatedly attest to God's matchless rule, especially in the enthronement psalms, which resound with the theme that the Lord reigns.
   2. God's sovereignty communicates His power over His enemies.
      a. Many Christians live as if the devil is sovereign, fearing the effects of his power and malice in their lives.
      b. However, though Satan's power is greater than ours, it is nothing compared to the might of our sovereign Lord.
   3. God's sovereignty establishes His power over our circumstances.
      a. Our future does not rest in the hands of human beings.
      b. Our destiny does not depend upon blind chance.
      c. Rather, God is actively involved in our lives, directing them according to His holy purposes.
   4. God's reign is not limited to past or future events; it permeates our present reality.
   5. God's reign is not limited to specific enclaves of Christian influence, but is cosmic in scope.

B. God's Eternal Purposes
   1. God's sovereign rule extends back to eternity.
   2. Ephesians 1:11 articulates God's eternal sovereignty in salvation, that Christians are "predestined according to the purpose of him who works all things according to the counsel of his will."
      a. The counsel of God refers to the inter-Trinitarian deliberation that preceded the creation of the universe.
      b. The will of God refers to His divine decisions and desires, which encompass and establish each aspect of our lives.
      c. The purpose of God refers to His divine determination to carry out His righteous will.
      d. God's act of predestination guarantees that His sovereign will is brought about in totality.

C. Arenas of Divine Sovereignty
   1. God's sovereignty governs creation.
      a. Everything that exists has God as its source.
      b. All things belong to God and exist for His glory.
      c. Plants, creatures, and the forces of nature are under God's complete control (Ps. 33:6–9).
   2. God's sovereignty governs history and providence.
      a. Rather than simply create things and set them in motion, God orders and directs human affairs (Ps. 33:10–11).

4—The Sovereignty of God

      b. In all circumstances, God is at work for the glory of His name and the good of His people (Rom. 8:28).
  3. God's sovereignty governs salvation.
      a. God predestines His people for salvation based on His eternal purposes, not His simple foreknowledge of human actions and decisions (Eph. 1:3–7).
      b. God's choice of His elect was made by Himself and for His glory.

STUDY QUESTIONS

1. Because the devil is stronger than we are, Christians are wise to fear him.
   a. True
   b. False

2. A factual understanding of divine sovereignty must recognize that _____.
   a. God in His sovereignty ordained that Satan would rebel against Him
   b. The devil only rarely thwarts God's purposes
   c. God will become fully sovereign once He defeats Satan
   d. God's power is vastly superior to Satan's power

3. Because God is sovereign, which of the following statements is false?
   a. The future ultimately does not rest in human hands.
   b. God's rule includes the past, present, and future.
   c. Humans have very little influence over their own lives.
   d. A Christian's destiny does not depend on blind chance.

4. Before the creation of the world, God chose to save certain individuals according to _____.
   a. His foreknowledge of those who would respond positively to the gospel
   b. The kind intention of His will
   c. Each individual's future works of love
   d. Their belonging to a faithful church

5. While it is true that God is sovereign over all, He nevertheless makes room where He withholds His influence so as to preserve the free choices of individual humans.
   a. True
   b. False

BIBLE STUDY AND DISCUSSION QUESTIONS

1. How can God's absolute sovereignty comfort those who are facing adversity? Is there a situation in your own life where you can find relief by meditating on God's sovereignty?

2. How does God's sovereignty over salvation keep Christians from relying on their own works?

3. Consider various churches that you have visited, or Christians with whom you have spoken. Do you see a correlation between their view of God's sovereignty and the way they speak about Him and live their lives?

4. How would you counsel another Christian who lives in fear of Satan and the forces of evil in this present world? Are there specific passages that would be instructive?

5

The Holiness of God

MESSAGE INTRODUCTION

To many people today, holiness is a foreign concept. For the authors of Scripture, however, holiness is one of God's most prominent attributes. It denotes both His separation from creation as the infinitely superior One and His absolute moral purity. In this lesson, Dr. Lawson explains what it means to affirm that God is holy, and how an understanding of this truth affects how we approach the living God and live before Him in humble reverence.

SCRIPTURE READINGS

Exodus 15:11; Isaiah 6:1–7

TEACHING OBJECTIVES

1. To explain what Scripture means when it calls God "holy"
2. To instill awe in the one who is exalted over all creation
3. To provide an impetus for the reverent sort of worship that God desires

QUOTATIONS

Infinite purity, even more than infinite knowledge or infinite power, is the object of reverence... "The Holy One of Israel" is He who is to be feared and adored.

—Charles Hodge

When the Bible calls God holy, it means primarily that God is transcendentally separate. He is so far above and beyond us that He seems almost totally foreign to us.

—R.C. Sproul

LECTURE OUTLINE

A. God's Surpassing Holiness
   1. God's holiness is uniquely emphasized in Scripture.
      a. The Bible repeatedly describes people, places, and things associated with God as "holy."
      b. The heavenly beings that surround God's throne continuously cry out, "Holy, holy, holy!"
      c. By describing God in this way, the angels are declaring that God is holy to a superlative degree, to be elevated and honored above all else.
   2. Of the many attributes used to describe God, holiness is one of the most prominent.
   3. Though Scripture often speaks of God's love, truth, and sovereignty, these other attributes are not presented with the same fanfare and trifold repetition.

B. God's Exalted Status
   1. To say that God is holy is to attest that He is separated above His creation.
      a. The Hebrew word translated into English as "holy" primarily indicates separation or the act of setting apart.
      b. God is therefore distinctly and infinitely superior to His creation and His creatures.
   2. To say that God is holy is to ascribe to Him kingly majesty (Ex. 15:11; Ps. 22:3).
      a. God's glory is too stunning for human beings to behold or comprehend.
      b. His royal splendor vastly exceeds that of the most exalted human monarchs.
   3. God's holiness is poignantly described in Isaiah 6:1–7.
      a. The train of God's royal robe is so extensive that it fills the temple.
      b. Even the dazzling seraphim—blazing in their intensity for God's glory—must cover themselves in the presence of God's splendor.
      c. Overwhelmed by this glimpse of God's holiness, Isaiah became profoundly aware of his own unclean and unworthy nature.
   4. The church is at its strongest when it recognizes and honors the holiness of God.

C. God's Moral Perfection
   1. God is completely without sin or moral blemish.
   2. All of God's decisions and judgments are perfect.
   3. As an infinitely holy being, God is not neutral toward good or evil.
      a. God takes delight in all that is true, worthy, and upright.
      b. Because God's very nature is one of purity, He cannot tolerate sin.
      c. It is only through the righteousness of Jesus Christ that guilty sinners can be reconciled to God.

STUDY QUESTIONS

1. The only divine attributes to be repeated three times in Scripture are holiness and love.
   a. True
   b. False

5—The Holiness of God

2. The Hebrew word translated into English as "holy" primarily expresses _____.
   a. Majesty
   b. Purity
   c. Moral excellence
   (d.) Separation

3. In Isaiah 6, the train of the Lord's robe symbolizes _____.
   a. His transcendence
   b. His authority
   (c.) His greatness
   d. His presence with His people

4. When we talk about God's holiness, we are referring primarily to his moral purity.
   a. True
   (b.) False

BIBLE STUDY AND DISCUSSION QUESTIONS

1. How does a proper understanding of God's holiness lead to a greater appreciation of His saving work? *God is revolted when he sees sin.*

2. How should a text like Isaiah 6 inform our worship in the church today? Is there any room for "casual" worship? *No.*

3. Scripture is often referred to as "Holy Scripture." How should a richer understanding of God's holiness affect how we read Scripture? *We should take His Word seriously.*

4. In his first epistle, Peter quotes Leviticus 11:44, which reads, "be holy, for I am holy." Read 1 Peter 1:13–21 and discuss how God's holiness ought to influence our manner of living.

- we should live a Holy life.

Note: when we share an idea + someone rejects it, we can so identify w/ the idea that we can become angry when its rejected.

It is a pride issue.

6

The Omnipresence of God

MESSAGE INTRODUCTION

As embodied beings, we are limited by space and time. When confronted with competing demands on our time, we often excuse ourselves by stating that we can't be in two places at once. God, however, can be in two places at once. In fact, He is everywhere at once. In this lesson, Dr. Lawson unfolds the biblical teaching of God's omnipresence, demonstrating that there is no place in heaven or hell, nor the entire universe, where God is not present in the fullness of His being.

SCRIPTURE READINGS

Psalm 139:7–10; Jeremiah 23:23–25

TEACHING OBJECTIVES

1. To explore the significance of God's unbounded presence
2. To correct misunderstandings about the nature of God's omnipresence
3. To demonstrate how an understanding of God's omnipresence can comfort Christians experiencing hardships

QUOTATIONS

If God be infinite, he is omnipresent. Suppose him infinite, and then suppose there is anything besides himself, and his presence with that thing, wherever it be, doth necessarily follow; for if he be so bounded as to be in his essence distant from anything, he is not infinite.
—John Owen

Does the Lord turn Himself unto our prayer only after long delay? Is not He omnipresent? Is not every whispered and stammering prayer known to Him, before there is yet a word in the tongue?

—Abraham Kuyper

6—The Omnipresence of God

LECTURE OUTLINE

A. Everywhere Present
1. The doctrine of divine omnipresence teaches that God is at the same time present in every part of the universe.
   a. As a spiritual being, God does not experience spatial constraints and is not barred from any location.
   b. Moreover, when God is present in all places, He is present in the fullness of His being.
2. The imagery of Psalm 139:7–10 encapsulates the comprehensive scope of God's presence.
   a. Whether one ascends to the highest point (heaven) or descends to the lowest point (Sheol), God is present.
   b. Whether one flees to the distant east (the wings of the morning) or to the distant west (the uttermost parts of the sea), God's presence and influence are there still.

B. The Heights of Heaven
1. God transcends human power and understanding.
2. Scripture attests that God rules from the highest place.
   a. The Lord is enthroned in the heavens (Ps. 123:1).
   b. God is exalted over all competitors, and He rules over all the earth (Ps. 97:9).
   c. God's throne is high and lifted up (Isa. 6:1).
   d. God's throne room is in heaven (Rev. 4:1–2).
3. Christians in all places and times can trust in the knowledge that their God is in absolute control and is actively at work in their lives.

C. Near the Earth
1. The God who is exalted on high (transcendent) is also present with His people (immanent).
2. Scripture affirms God's commitment to His creation and His people.
   a. God accompanies His people in the valley of the shadow of death (Ps. 23:4).
   b. God is present on earth and in heaven (Deut. 4:39).
   c. God dwells both in the high places and with the humble and lowly (Isa. 57:15).
   d. God will be with His children to the end of the age (Matt. 28:20), never leaving or forsaking them (Heb. 13:5).

D. The Depths of Hell
1. It is God Himself who administers divine wrath in hell.
   a. Revelation 14:10 describes eternal punishment taking place "in the presence of the holy angels and in the presence of the Lamb."

b. Although hell is sometimes described as a place where God is absent, He will be all too real to those who experience His judgment there.

c. Despite being present in hell, God will turn His countenance—His gaze of blessing—away from hell's inhabitants.

E. Concluding Thoughts
1. The doctrine of God's omnipresence offers tremendous encouragement.
   a. God is with us in the midst of trial and adversity.
   b. God is committed to His people.
   c. Since God alone is omnipresent, Satan is spatially finite and must rely upon his minions to wage spiritual warfare.
2. The doctrine of divine omnipresence also offers a grave warning.
   a. Those who oppose God can never flee from Him.
   b. Those who experience God's common grace but do not respond in faith will one day experience only divine wrath.

STUDY QUESTIONS

1. Hell is the one place where God withholds His presence.
   a. True
   b. False

2. The Latin word *omni* means _____.
   a. Present
   b. Powerful
   c. Unlimited
   d. All

3. Concerning God's omnipresence, all of the following are true *except* _____.
   a. He is equally accessible to all believers at all times
   b. The grave cannot separate individuals from Him
   c. At the incarnation, the Son of God gave up His ability to be present everywhere
   d. His sovereignty includes both His immanence and His transcendence

4. It is Satan who carries out vengeance on the unbeliever in hell.
   a. True
   b. False

BIBLE STUDY AND DISCUSSION QUESTIONS

1. At the beginning of the lesson, Dr. Lawson quotes Richard Sibbes, who said, "How shall the finite comprehend the infinite? We shall apprehend Him but not comprehend Him." What does it mean to apprehend but not comprehend God?

2. In what ways is God's omnipresence great news for believers and terrifying news for unbelievers?

3. In a previous lesson on God's sovereignty, Dr. Lawson mentioned that many Christians live in fear of Satan. How can a proper understanding of God's omnipresence help to overcome this fear?

4. Is there a time in your own life when you have felt particularly distant from God? How can you understand such an experience in light of this lesson?

7

The Omniscience of God

MESSAGE INTRODUCTION

When reflecting on the limited capacity of the human mind, it is difficult to fathom a being who knows everything perfectly. There are some today who would limit God's knowledge, arguing that it interferes with the free choices of individuals, but this runs counter to the clear and consistent teaching of Scripture. In this message, Dr. Lawson considers what it means to affirm that God is omniscient and why this aspect of His character is essential to our understanding of who He is.

SCRIPTURE READINGS

Isaiah 46:8–10; Romans 11:33–36

TEACHING OBJECTIVES

1. To consider the height, depth, length, and breadth of God's omniscience
2. To explain how God's exhaustive knowledge ought to both comfort and convict
3. To impart humility in light of God's limitless understanding

QUOTATIONS

In public, in private; [God] knows all cases, and he knows all remedies; he knows the seasons of bringing them, and he knows the seasons of removing them, for his own glory. What is contingent in respect of us, and of our foreknowledge, and in respect of second causes, is not so in regard of God's . . . he knows all causes in themselves, and, therefore, knows what every cause will produce, what will be the event of every counsel and of every action.

—Stephen Charnock

7—The Omniscience of God

Lord, how terrible is Thine omniscience for Thine enemies. That eye which burns in heaven as a flame of fire is always upon them. They would fain flee away from it, but they are never able. But for Thy people, Thine omniscience is a comfort and a refuge. Thou art He who can help them against themselves and the deceitfulness of their own hearts. They invite Thine omniscience to search their heart and to cleanse them from their secret faults.

—Andrew Murray

LECTURE OUTLINE

A. Perfect Self-Knowledge
   1. God's omniscience includes perfect knowledge of Himself, the triune Godhead.
   2. The three persons of the Trinity know each other fully, with no gaps in their knowledge (Matt. 11:27; John 10:15).
   3. Though no human can fathom the thoughts of God, He knows them completely (1 Cor. 2:11).

B. Perfect Knowledge
   1. God knows all things as they truly are.
      a. God never learns anything new.
      b. Nothing ever surprises God or takes Him off guard.
      c. God is not prone to confusion or misunderstanding.
   2. There is no darkness in God's knowledge (1 John 1:5).
   3. When we bring our petitions and requests before God, we know that His responses are grounded in His all-encompassing knowledge.

C. Eternal Knowledge
   1. Human knowledge is gained through a succession of experiences.
   2. Humans can forget what they know.
   3. God, on the other hand, has known all things from before the foundation of the world, and this knowledge remains intact forever (Isa. 46:8–10).
   4. God not only knows the outcome of history, but He is also familiar with every human thought and action throughout history.

D. Immediate Knowledge
   1. God knows all things instantly and simultaneously.
   2. God has never needed anyone to instruct or counsel Him (Rom. 11:34; Isa. 40:13–14).

E. Exhaustive Knowledge
   1. God's knowledge encompasses minute details.
      a. He numbers and names the stars (Ps. 147:4).
      b. He counts the hairs on a person's head, and not even a sparrow falls apart from the Lord's knowledge (Matt. 10:29–30).

2. God knows unseen details about our lives, and there is nothing that we can hide from Him.

F. Penetrating Knowledge
1. God's knowledge penetrates the depths of the human heart.
2. He knows us far more intimately than we know ourselves (Ps. 139:1–4).
3. Even though God is fully acquainted with the depths of our sin and depravity, He does not withhold His love and forgiveness from us.

G. Future Knowledge
1. God knows the future because He has foreordained whatever shall come to pass.
2. God's knowledge of future events sets Him apart from lifeless idols.

H. Possible Knowledge
1. God knows not only the reality of what is, but also the possibility of other things that might have been.
2. He is aware of the potential consequences of every possible human action that ever could have been taken (Matt. 11:21, 23).

STUDY QUESTIONS

1. Since Luke states that Jesus grew in wisdom (Luke 2:52), we can infer that God is always increasing in knowledge.
    a. True
    b. False

2. God's "immediate knowledge" primarily refers to _____.
    a. His simultaneous knowledge of everything
    b. His knowledge specifically in the present
    c. His knowledge of the thoughts of individuals
    d. His knowledge of the future

3. Concerning God's omniscience, which of the following statements is false?
    a. Since God knows everything, humans can't be responsible for their own actions.
    b. God's knowledge includes the past, present, and future.
    c. Humans are dependent upon God for true knowledge of Him.
    d. The fall of mankind in Genesis 3 did not surprise God.

4. God knows us even better than we know ourselves.
    a. True
    b. False

BIBLE STUDY AND DISCUSSION QUESTIONS

1. How should the fact that only God has perfect self-knowledge influence how we come to know Him? Can we come to know Him through our own effort?

2. Dr. Lawson stresses that nothing ever catches God off guard. How does this bring relief to Christians in difficult circumstances? Does the fact that He knows everything provide comfort by itself, or does comfort come from considering His knowledge together with other attributes?

3. Since God knows ahead of time what will be asked of Him in prayer, what is accomplished by praying?

4. Dr. Lawson states that God's exhaustive knowledge is both comforting and convicting. In what way is it comforting? In what way is it convicting?

8

The Omnipotence of God

MESSAGE INTRODUCTION

Like all of His attributes, God's omnipotence is co-extensive with His being. There is no area of the universe where He is not exerting His power. From a blade of grass to the stars of the sky, everything and everyone is dependent upon His immeasurable power for its existence. In this lesson, Dr. Lawson explores the nature and extent of this incomprehensible power.

SCRIPTURE READINGS

Isaiah 40:28–31; Ephesians 3:20–21

TEACHING OBJECTIVES

1. To show the extent of God's power
2. To commend worship of the One who controls all events at all times
3. To instill humility by considering our frailty in light of God's limitless power

QUOTATIONS

But however strong may be the purposes either of angels or of men, whether of good or bad, whether these purposes fall in with the will of God or run counter to it, the will of the Omnipotent is never defeated.

—Augustine of Hippo

We can do very little. God can do whatever He wills. We, beyond very narrow limits, must use means to accomplish our ends. With God means are unnecessary. He wills, and it is done. He said, Let there be light; and there was light. He, by a volition created the heavens and the earth. At the volition of Christ, the winds ceased, and there was a great calm. By an act of the will He healed the sick, opened the eyes of the blind, and raised the dead. This simple idea of the omnipotence of God, that He can do without effort, and by a volition, whatever He wills, is the highest conceivable idea of power, and is that which is clearly presented in the Scriptures.

—Charles Hodge

LECTURE OUTLINE

A. Infinite Power
   1. God possesses all power.
      a. All human power and ability ultimately belongs to God.
      b. Even Satan's power is allotted to him by God.
      c. Moreover, when God is present in all places, He is present in the fullness of His being.
   2. God's power is without limits or bounds.
      a. He has the means to carry out His every desire.
      b. Nothing is too difficult for God to accomplish (Jer. 32:27).
      c. God is able to do what humans cannot, including the act of saving sinners.
   3. The knowledge that God can overcome all obstacles should encourage us to pray to Him boldly and persistently.

B. Irresistible Power
   1. No one can thwart, resist, or undermine God's purposes (Job 42:2; Isa. 14:27; Isa. 43:13).
   2. God does not have to struggle to bring about His will.
      a. God does not depend upon human action to achieve His goals.
      b. The battle between God and Satan is not a stalemate or a tug-of-war.
      c. God effortlessly prevails over human rebellion and Satanic resistance.

C. Inexhaustible Power
   1. God's power does not diminish over time.
   2. He never grows weary or tired (Isa. 40:28).
   3. Through His inexhaustible energy, He gives strength to His people (Isa. 40:29–31).
   4. Scripture assures believers that they can do all things through the strengthening power of Jesus Christ (Phil. 4:13).
      a. As we trust in Christ, He exchanges our weakness for His strength.
      b. God's inexhaustible strength empowers us to carry out what He calls us to do.

D. Incomprehensible Power
   1. God's power is so far beyond human capabilities that we simply cannot understand it.
   2. God is "able to do far more abundantly than all that we ask or think" (Eph. 3:20).
   3. God works in human hearts in unseen and mysterious ways.

E. Self-Consistent Power
   1. God's power works in perfect conformity with all of His other attributes.

2. Due to God's nature, there are certain things that He cannot do.
   a. God cannot act inconsistently with His holiness, love, immutability, or other qualities.
   b. This is not an ontological limitation of God's power; rather, it demonstrates the boundless nature of each of His attributes.

STUDY QUESTIONS

1. Even the power that Satan possesses comes from God.
   a. True
   b. False

2. God's omnipotence works most closely with His _____.
   a. Sovereignty
   b. Omnipresence
   c. Omniscience
   d. All of the above

3. Because God is omnipotent, all of the following are true *except* _____.
   a. God's power is incomprehensible
   b. God's power is like ours, but it is quantitatively greater
   c. God's power influences human choices
   d. God's power is present everywhere in the same degree

4. Since God is all-powerful and can do whatever He pleases, He is free to change His mind with respect to who will be saved.
   a. True
   b. False

BIBLE STUDY AND DISCUSSION QUESTIONS

1. Consider how any power that you possess has been delegated to you from God. How should this affect your relationships with others, whether in the workplace, the family, or among friends?

2. Have you known individuals who have exhibited extreme hostility toward the gospel? How can a consideration of God's omnipotence provide encouragement when you pray for or witness to them?

3. How should knowing that every moment of your existence is dependent on God influence how you spend your time? How should this bring humility to life's pursuits?

4. Does God's omnipotence in and of itself provide you comfort? Or is it only in conjunction with His other attributes? Does this say anything about the benefits or dangers of elevating one aspect of His character to the exclusion of others?

9

The Immutability of God

MESSAGE INTRODUCTION

It is hard for anyone to go a day, even an hour, without changing in some way. Our thoughts and emotions are in a constant state of flux. Even our greatest desires and plans change over time. God, however, never changes His mind or His course of action in the world. He is an immovable rock, a mighty fortress, and the only sure anchor in an ever-changing world. In this lesson, Dr. Lawson explores the biblical view of God's immutability, showing how His character, Word, plan, and salvation never change.

SCRIPTURE READINGS

Psalm 102:25–28; Isaiah 14:26–27

TEACHING OBJECTIVES

1. To explain the nature of God's immutability and how it affects the Christian's life
2. To encourage reliance upon Him who never changes
3. To inspire praise for the One whose eternal and glorious plan will never be thwarted

QUOTATIONS

The greatest and only consolation of Christians in their adversities, is the knowing that God lies not, but does all things immutably, and that His will cannot be resisted, changed, or hindered.

—Martin Luther

However unstable I may be, however fickle my friends may prove, God changes not. If He varied as we do, if He willed one thing today and another tomorrow, if He were controlled by caprice, who could confide in Him? But, all praise to His glorious name, He is ever the same. His purpose is fixed, His will is stable, His word is sure.

—A.W. Pink

LECTURE OUTLINE

A. Unchangeable in Character
   1. God's personality is eternal and unalterable.
      a. He never increases or decreases (Ps. 102:26–27).
      b. All of God's attributes are constant and steadfast.
   2. We have Scripture's guarantee that the God whom we serve is the same each day.
      a. Though our lives unfold in various stages, the same God is with us throughout.
      b. When we lift our prayers to Him, we do not have to anticipate divine inconsistency or mood swings.
      c. Moreover, when God is present in all places, He is present in the fullness of His being.

B. Unchangeable in Word
   1. God's Word can never be altered or abridged.
   2. God's Word cannot fail to come to pass.
   3. God neither lies nor takes back what He has said (Num. 23:19).
      a. Fallen human beings, on the other hand, tend to twist the truth, change their minds, or mislead others intentionally or unintentionally.
      b. Even human laws change, but God's Word stands forever (Isa. 40:8).
   4. Jesus taught that it would be easier for heaven and earth to pass away than for a single stroke of God's law to fail to be accomplished (Luke 16:17).
   5. In all generations, God's standards are the same, and His plan of salvation is the same.

C. Unchangeable in Plans
   1. God's eternal decrees can never be altered.
   2. He is never forced to change His plans or adopt a "Plan B."
   3. God's purposes override and encompass human plans (Ps. 33:10–11; Prov. 19:21).
   4. No one can frustrate or annul God's plans (Isa. 14:26–27).

D. Unchangeable in Salvation
   1. Though God's redemptive work advances throughout human history, His plan of salvation has remained unchanged.
   2. From eternity, God has set apart His elect, and He will not reject or fail to save even one of His children.
   3. The spiritual rebirth that believers experience is a new birth unto eternal life and is not a merely short-term sample of divine favor.
   4. God's promises to believers are given unconditionally and with absolute certainty.

A divine intention can be changed. — conditional on what you do.
A divine decree cannot be changed.

9—The Immutability of God

We change & can move into a different category. Change in the relations w/ man

STUDY QUESTIONS

1. While it is true to say that God does not change with respect to His being, He is nevertheless able to adjust His plan in history so as to bring more glory to Himself.
   a. True
   b. <u>False</u>

2. Put the following events in the order that they appear in Romans 8:29–30.
   - _4_ He justified
   - _3_ He called
   - _2_ He predestined
   - _5_ He glorified
   - _1_ He foreknew

3. Which of these is not correct?
   a. Immutability relates to God's character.
   b. Immutability means that the number of those saved will neither increase nor decrease.
   c. <u>Immutability is best understood apart from God's other attributes.</u>
   d. Immutability also applies to God's Word.

4. Malachi 3:6 states that the sons of Jacob are not consumed because of God's mercy.
   a. True
   b. <u>False</u>

BIBLE STUDY AND DISCUSSION QUESTIONS

1. If God never changes, how is it that our relationship with Him can change over time? *We mature in our faith*

2. How should reflection on the unchangeableness of God's plan, including His plan for your life, lead you to thanksgiving when things go well and comfort you when they do not? *God's plan is for our well-being & benefit.*

3. How can Christians affirm God's immutability in light of the incarnation of the Son of God? <u>Did the Son not change when He became man?</u>

4. How does God's unchangeableness with respect to His Word inspire confidence in your study of Scripture?
   God's word is reliable, consistent, & unchanging.

10

The Truthfulness of God

MESSAGE INTRODUCTION

In an age when truth is often seen as entirely subjective, the Bible's presentation of a God whose truthfulness is absolute and objective stands in stark contrast. Moreover, the claim that this God has spoken truth in sacred Scripture stands the wisdom of this world on its head. In this lesson, Dr. Lawson examines several aspects of the truthfulness of God, showing why it is such a radical and countercultural view to hold in today's world.

SCRIPTURE READINGS

John 14:6; 17:17–19

TEACHING OBJECTIVES

1. To explain the multifaceted richness of God's truthfulness
2. To instill trust in the truthfulness of God's word
3. To contrast the Christian and secular views of truth

QUOTATIONS

The truth of God is a great pillar for our faith. Were not he a God of truth, how could we believe in him? Our faith were fancy; but he is truth itself, and not a word which he has spoken shall fall to the ground.

—Thomas Watson

Truth holds together. Therefore, there is no phase of truth that is not related to every other phase of truth. All things that are true are part of the truth and stand in a proper and inescapable relationship to God, who is himself the truth.

—James Montgomery Boice

LECTURE OUTLINE

A. Divine Truth
   1. All truth has its origin in God.
      a. Truth is defined by God's very nature.
      b. Humanity has access to truth only through God's revelation.
   2. God not only speaks truth; He *is* truth (John 14:6).
   3. Though God appoints human teachers for His people, it is ultimately the Spirit of truth who instructs the people of God (John 15:26; 16:13).

B. Absolute Truth
   1. Truth makes exclusive claims about reality.
   2. Though the Bible at times speaks of *a* truth, it nevertheless also speaks of *the* truth.
   3. Truth establishes a firm boundary between right and wrong, factual and fabricated.

C. Objective Truth
   1. Truth presents specific propositions and claims.
   2. God's Word is true even down to its most minute details.
      a. Certain statements in Scripture are of greater importance than others.
      b. Yet, all of Scripture's claims are true, regardless of the subject matter.
   3. God's words are inherently true and do not depend on human understanding or feelings.

D. Singular Truth
   1. Truth stands as a single body.
      a. Truth does not compete with itself or contradict itself.
      b. God exists in complete harmony with himself.
      c. Scripture expresses a unified system of reality.
   2. God's revelation to humanity is consistent.
      a. He does not say something to one group and something else to another group.
      b. God does not reveal different paths of salvation to different people.
      c. God's Word communicates a unified message that applies to all people, places, and times.

E. Immutable Truth
   1. Just as God does not change, His truth does not change.
   2. No part of Scripture will ever be annulled or removed.
   3. God's words to humanity are always relevant and up to date.

F. Universal Truth
   1. Truth transcends societies, cultures, centuries, and continents.
   2. Truth does not change to accommodate one's worldview, surroundings, or social norms.
   3. All people need to hear and obey God's truth.

G. Illuminating Truth
   1. Truth enables us to understand the world around us and perceive things as they actually are (Ps. 119:105).
   2. Apart from God's Word, humanity remains in darkness and in a state of spiritual blindness.

H. Trustworthy Truth
   1. God's words are utterly reliable and dependable.
   2. God does not mislead people or lead them down the path of falsehood.
   3. Those who believe and live according to the truth base their lives on a firm foundation.

I. Authoritative Truth
   1. Because God is the source of truth, He has the power to assert claims and make demands upon human beings.
      a. Truth is never merely a collection of interesting information.
      b. Rather, it requires a human response of obedience.
   2. God's people are to "be doers of the word, and not hearers only" (James 1:22).
   3. Truth is essential.
      a. In order to live well as God's people in the world, we must understand things as they truly are.
      b. Our salvation involves hearing and responding to the truth of Scripture (Rom. 10:13–17).

STUDY QUESTIONS

1. Since Satan is the antithesis of truth, it can be said that he never utters true statements.
   a. True
   b. False

2. Since truth is absolute, all of the following are true *except*_____.
   a. One truth cannot be more important than another
   b. Truth cannot contradict itself
   c. Scripture will never become untrue
   d. The gospel message must be the same to every culture

3. Because the Bible is trustworthy, all of the following are true *except* _____.
   a. Its truth will never be overturned
   b. Its truth depends on proper interpretation
   c. It is true for all people and for all time
   d. It makes scientific inquiry pointless

4. Those who don't have access to Scripture cannot be held responsible for acting contrary to Scripture, because they don't know of its authoritative status.
   a. True
   b. False

BIBLE STUDY AND DISCUSSION QUESTIONS

1. If Pilate had waited for a response from Jesus when he asked Him what truth was, how do you think Jesus would have responded?

2. Consider Dr. Lawson's point that truth is singular, forming "one perfect tapestry of truth." How should this affect one's interpretation of difficult passages in Scripture?

3. In a time when the Bible is often attacked as containing mythology and contradictions, how can you help fellow believers to hold fast to its trustworthiness? How can you challenge unbelievers in this respect?

4. If someone were to tell you that they respect your religious beliefs but that those beliefs are not true for them, how would you respond?

11

The Wisdom of God

MESSAGE INTRODUCTION

The thought that the brutal execution of a Jewish man in first-century Palestine could be the means by which God brings salvation to mankind is considered foolishness by the world. But it was in this very event that God demonstrated His infinite and unsearchable wisdom. In this message, Dr. Lawson provides a biblical definition of wisdom and examines God's wisdom in creation, providence, and salvation.

SCRIPTURE READINGS

Isaiah 55:8–9; Romans 11:33–34; 1 Corinthians 1:18–25

TEACHING OBJECTIVES

1. To explain what wisdom is, and to show where God's wisdom is most clearly revealed
2. To show how God's wisdom ought to comfort believers who are facing difficulties or confusion
3. To commend God's infinite wisdom as an invitation to greater worship

QUOTATIONS

We must suffer God to be wiser than ourselves, and acknowledge that there is something sovereign in his ways not to be measured by the feeble reed of our weak understandings.

—Stephen Charnock

The wisdom of God in [the work of redemption] is of vast extent. The contrivance is so manifold, that one may spend an eternity in discovering more of the excellent ends and designs accomplished by it; and the multitude and vast variety of things that are, by divine contrivance, brought to conspire to the bringing about of those ends.

—Jonathan Edwards

LECTURE OUTLINE

A. Definition of God's Wisdom
   1. Wisdom is the pursuit of the highest purpose and the greatest good.
      a. In all situations, the highest and wisest goal is the glory of God and the good of His people.
      b. Wisdom begins with the fear of the Lord (Ps. 111:10; Prov. 9:10).
      c. Wisdom includes both the goal and the means to achieving that goal.
   2. God, who is all-wise, always chooses the highest end and the best means to that end.
      a. In all circumstances, He is at work for the glory of His name and the good of His people.
      b. Because God is all-powerful, it is significant that His might is constantly employed for the highest purposes.

B. God's Wisdom in Creation
   1. One of the major arenas where God's wisdom can be seen is in His creative acts and the things He has made.
      a. The sky and the heavens proclaim God's glory through their majesty and splendor (Ps. 19:1–6).
      b. John Calvin described the earth as a theater where God's wisdom and power are always on display.
      c. The world, in its intricate beauty, illustrates certain aspects of God's character (Rom. 1:20).
   2. Even God's means of bringing the universe into existence was in keeping with His power and glory.
   3. The order and design of the created order demonstrate the wisdom of its Creator.
      a. The angle and rotation of the earth was perfectly engineered to promote the flourishing of living things on this planet.
      b. The regularity of the winds, tides, and seasons attests to God's power and genius.

C. God's Wisdom in Providence
   1. With His glory as the goal, God orchestrates human circumstances so as to bring about this highest end.
      a. God sovereignly and wisely arranges the specific details of each person's life (Acts 17:26–27).

  b. Though we may not understand why certain aspects of our lives are the way they are, Scripture affirms that God works through all circumstances to achieve His purposes in us.
  c. In His wisdom, God uses trials and difficulties to draw His children closer to Himself and to make them more like Jesus Christ.
 2. Often, seemingly dark and hopeless circumstances later reveal God's sovereign wisdom at work.
  a. Though Joseph's brothers intended evil against him, God intended that their actions would bring about good (Gen. 50:20).
  b. The crucifixion of Jesus Christ was the greatest evil ever committed, but God predetermined that Christ's death would bring about His perfect plan of salvation.
 3. In all situations, God is wisely carrying out His master plan for the glory of His name and the good of His people.

D. God's Wisdom in Salvation
 1. God's plan of salvation is both simple enough to explain to a child and intricate enough to defy the wisdom of the most brilliant human minds.
  a. Through Christ's law-keeping, our law-breaking is pardoned.
  b. Because God's wrath and curse fell upon the innocent, the guilty experience God's favor and blessing.
  c. Amid His apparent defeat by sin and death, Christ won a decisive victory over the powers of darkness.
 2. Even though God's redemptive plan may appear to be folly to those who have earthly wisdom, God "chose what is foolish in the world to shame the wise" (1 Cor. 1:27).

STUDY QUESTIONS

1. Even works of evil and hatred are a part of God's wise plan.
 a. True
 b. False

2. God's wisdom is best described as _____.
 a. His knowledge of everything
 b. The purity of His thoughts
 c. His choice of the highest end and the best means to that end
 d. The quality of His knowledge that distinguishes His thoughts from man's

3. Because God is ultimately wise, all of the following are true *except* _____.
 a. The history of the world will lead to His glory
 b. His wise choices will always be comprehensible to people
 c. Studying the natural world reveals His wisdom
 d. His providential choices will always have their desired end

11—The Wisdom of God

4. God's wisdom is best displayed in the works of nature.
   a. True
   b. False

BIBLE STUDY AND DISCUSSION QUESTIONS

1. How can meditating on God's wisdom help you or someone you know to be comforted when reflecting on the difficulties of life, both past and present?

2. Many people, even those who claim not to be religious, find their emotions stirred when viewing nature. How can you use opportunities like these to point them to the God whose wisdom created the natural world?

3. Are there times in your life when it feels like God did *not* choose the best means to accomplish His glorifying end? How can considering the wisdom of the cross, which is foolishness to the world (1 Cor. 1:18), bring clarity and renewed trust in His plan?

4. How should your everyday decisions be affected by a consideration of God's wisdom and the final goal to which His wisdom is directed?

- Hard to believe - book
- The Star of Bethlehem - movie
  - Netflix

12

The Goodness of God

MESSAGE INTRODUCTION

It is not uncommon for those who face pain and hardship in this life to doubt the goodness of God. But the clear message of Scripture is that God is uniquely good, and that He is the measure for everything we call good. Considered together with His wisdom and power, Christians can be assured that God not only desires to reveal His goodness, but is able to accomplish His good plan in the best possible way. In this lesson, Dr. Lawson explores what it means to say that God is good, and how His goodness is operative in the world.

SCRIPTURE READINGS

Psalm 145:8–17; James 1:16–18

TEACHING OBJECTIVES

1. To explain the nature and extent of God's goodness
2. To encourage those who struggle with God's goodness in the face of adversity
3. To elicit praise for the God who alone is good

QUOTATIONS

God the Father has not only given us all that we have and see before our eyes, but daily preserves and defends us against all evil and misfortune, averts all sorts of danger and calamity; and that He does all this out of pure love and goodness, without our merit, as a benevolent Father, who cares for us that no evil befall us.

—Martin Luther

12—The Goodness of God

The goodness of God . . . is the loveliness, benign character, sweetness, friendliness, kindness, and generosity of God. Goodness is the very essence of God's Being, even if there were no creature to whom this could be manifested.

—Wilhelmus à Brakel

LECTURE OUTLINE

A. God Is Good to All Creatures
  1. God's abundant goodness permeates the entire created order (Pss. 136:25; 145:9, 15–16).
  2. God's goodness extends even to the animal kingdom (Matt. 6:26; Job 38:41).

B. God Is Good to Unbelievers
  1. God extends to all people what is called "common grace"—His general goodness which is not redemptive (Matt. 5:45).
  2. Unbelievers are allowed to marry, have children, work, advance in their careers, etc.
  3. Unbelievers are able to enjoy the beauty of God's creation (Acts 14:17).
  4. Unbelievers can experience so much of God's goodness that it can sometimes appear like He's being better to them than to His own children (Ps. 73).

C. God Is Good to His Children
  1. There are general aspects of God's goodness to His children.
      a. The goodness God lavishes on His children is not always in the form of material abundance, but any abundance does come from Him.
      b. God delights in meeting the needs of His children (Matt. 7:7).
      c. Everything good ultimately comes from God (James 1:17).
  2. There are specific aspects of God's goodness towards His children.
      a. God is good in His plans for believers (Rom. 12:2; Jer. 29:11; Eph. 2:10). Even trials are used to conform believers to the image of Christ.
      b. God is good toward believers with respect to His providence (Rom. 8:28).
      c. God is good in His protection of believers (Nah. 1:7).
      d. God is good in His patience toward believers.
      e God is good in His forgiveness toward believers.
  3. Believers should never doubt God's goodness. Getting believers to doubt God's goodness is one of Satan's greatest ploys.

STUDY QUESTIONS

1. Since God is good, everyone can expect that their life will ultimately turn out for their own good.
    a. True
    b. False

2. Because God is good, which of the following statements is incorrect?
   a. He uses difficult circumstances in our lives to conform us to the image of Christ.
   b. Even the wicked benefit from His goodness.
   c. He cares for even the smallest details of the natural world.
   d. He will always protect His people from physical harm.

3. In Psalm 73, Asaph gained a new perspective on the wealth and ease of the wicked by _____.
   a. Visiting the poor
   b. Talking with fellow believers
   c. Reading the Bible
   d. Going to the house of the Lord

4. Since God wills to send unbelievers to hell, it cannot be said that He is good to them.
   a. True
   b. False

BIBLE STUDY AND DISCUSSION QUESTIONS

1. If circumstances in your life cause you to doubt God's goodness, where in Scripture can you turn for reassurance and confidence?

2. Which of God's other attributes can assure you that God is *able* to exercise His goodness? Can you think of more than one?

3. Romans 8:28 states, "For those who love God all things work together for good." Can you think of difficult experiences in your past when you doubted the wisdom and goodness of His plan, but which turned out for good?

4. How can you help unbelievers to see that their lives have been affected by the goodness of God? How would you conduct such a conversation?

Handwritten notes:

Ray Comfort - look on Youtube

manifestation of goodness can vary based on circumstances.
judge - rendering verdict to criminal
   - judge is still good.

13

The Grace of God

MESSAGE INTRODUCTION

When asked to summarize the law, Jesus responded that one must love God and neighbor. Considering the grace of God ought to help believers fulfill both commandments. God's grace should both flood one's heart with thankfulness and love for Him, and also provide the model for how we should treat our neighbor. In this lesson, Dr. Lawson uncovers the extent of God's grace, which is seen most clearly in the salvation accomplished in His Son.

SCRIPTURE READINGS

1 Corinthians 15:10; Titus 2:11–15

TEACHING OBJECTIVES

1. To explain the character of God's incomparable grace
2. To show the unworthiness of man to receive God's grace
3. To commend the grace of God which ought to lead to thankfulness and worship

QUOTATIONS

Faith is a living, unshakeable confidence in God's grace; it is so certain, that someone would die a thousand times for it. This kind of trust in and knowledge of God's grace makes a person joyful, confident, and happy with regard to God and all creatures.

—Martin Luther

Repentance was never yet produced in any man's heart apart from the grace of God. As soon may you expect the leopard to regret the blood with which its fangs are moistened—as soon might you expect the lion of the wood to abjure his cruel tyranny over the feeble beasts of the plain, as expect the sinner to make any confession, or offer any repentance that shall be accepted of God, unless grace shall first renew the heart.

—Charles Spurgeon

LECTURE OUTLINE

A. God's Grace Is Free
   1. The gospel of Jesus Christ is a gift that God offers and extends to those who are guilty.
   2. Grace and works cannot mix.
      a. If works play a role in justification, then God's grace is no longer grace (Rom. 11:6).
      b. Ephesians 2:9 states that salvation is "not a result of works, so that no one may boast."

B. God's Grace Is Eternal
   1. Before time began, God planned to give His grace to His elect.
      a. The elect were not chosen on the basis of what they would do.
      b. They were chosen according to God's own purpose and grace (2 Tim. 1:9)

C. God's Grace Is Sovereign
   1. God did not have to choose to be gracious to anyone.
   2. No one has a claim on the grace of God because it's given to those who are undeserving (Ex. 33:19).

D. God's Grace Is Far Reaching
   1. It is extended to and made real in the lives of all kinds of people around the globe (Titus 2:11).
   2. This includes men and women, Jews and Gentiles, slave and free, educated and uneducated, and people from all languages and cultures.

E. God's Grace Is Mediated
   1. It is mediated through the Lord Jesus Christ (1 Tim. 2:5)
      a. There is *no* salvation outside of Christ (Rom. 5:15).
      b. Christ alone can represent man to God and God to man, since He is fully God and fully man.
   2. To have Christ is to have everything; not to have Christ is to have nothing.

F. God's Grace Is Saving
   1. God's grace saves believers from God Himself. Apart from His grace, mankind can only expect His judgment and wrath.
   2. God's saving grace is super-abounding. There is no amount of sin that God's grace cannot overcome (Rom. 5:20).
   3. God's saving grace is transformative. By it, He transforms believers into the image of Christ (2 Cor. 3:18).

*all are save - doesn't mean all w/o exception
means all w/o distinction of races*

STUDY QUESTIONS

1. Because salvation is a gift of God's grace, works are unimportant.
   a. True
   b. False

2. Because God is gracious, which of the following statements is false?
   a. His grace overcomes the hearts of the wicked.
   b. There is no amount of sin that He cannot forgive.
   c. He will not ultimately judge the wicked.
   d. Humans must respond with thanksgiving.

3. Since God's grace is mediated, which of the following statements is false?
   a. Christ is the mediator between God and man.
   b. There is no salvation outside of Christ.
   c. The church is unimportant.
   d. Other religions can experience His grace through different mediators.

4. Because God's grace is sovereign, no one can resist it.
   a. True
   b. False

BIBLE STUDY AND DISCUSSION QUESTIONS

1. Reflect on the first time you became aware that salvation is purely a gift of God's grace, apart from any works. How did you respond to God?

2. There are many people who believe they will experience a pleasant afterlife on account of their having been a good person. How could you give a biblical response to such a person?

3. Are there times in your life when you've felt that your sins were too great to be forgiven? What passages of Scripture address such situations?

4. How should a consideration of God's free and sovereign grace influence Christian worship? How should it affect Christian relationships?

14

The Love of God

MESSAGE INTRODUCTION

Love is a word that is frequently thrown around without consideration of what it truly means. It is often thought of as feeling or attraction, but Scripture provides a much more profound understanding of what love is. Furthermore, it is God's love that provides the exemplar for all derivative forms of love. In this lesson, Dr. Lawson explores the depths of God's love, which is an infinite and eternally self-giving love.

SCRIPTURE READINGS

1 John 4:7–12; John 17:20–26

TEACHING OBJECTIVES

1. To discuss the implications of God's eternal and self-giving love
2. To recognize our inability to comprehend God's immeasurable love
3. To invite Christians to take refuge in the Father's love

QUOTATIONS

God's love is the most awesome thing about Him. It is not His justice, nor His majesty, nor even His blazing holiness, but the fact that He has made and keeps a covenant of personal commitment and love to His people.

—Sinclair B. Ferguson

Christ opens up the first cause, and, as it were, the source of our salvation, and he does so, that no doubt may remain; for our minds cannot find calm repose, until we arrive at the unmerited love of God.

—John Calvin

God's love was sacrificial for what we would ultimately do - worshipping Him.

LECTURE OUTLINE

A. God's Love Is Intra-Trinitarian Love
1. The love God shows toward humanity is a love that first existed within the Godhead (John 3:35).
2. As the Father has loved the Son, even so He has now loved believers (John 17:26).

B. God's Love Is Infinite
1. When Christ comes to live inside Christians, He brings the Father's infinite love with Him.

C. God's Love Is Sacrificial
1. True love is a love that gives.
2. This is most powerfully seen in the Father's giving His only Son to redeem sinners (Rom. 5:8).
3. As the good shepherd who lays His life down for His sheep, Christ laid down His life for the lost (John 10:11).

D. God's Love Is Volitional
1. It is a choice of God's will.
2. He chose His people not because of something inherently worthy of love in them (Deut. 7:7).
3. God is the initiator and pursuer in His relationship with individuals (1 John 4:19).

E. God's Love Is Eternal
1. There is no beginning or end to His love (Jer. 31:3).
2. Predestination expresses the greatest love that there has ever been.
   a. It is the love of the Father for His chosen ones as He eternally loved and elected (Eph. 1:4–5).

F. God's Love Is Passionate
1. God's heart is full of affection for His people (Deut. 30:9; Isa. 64:4).

STUDY QUESTIONS

1. Of the following words, the one that best describes a scriptural view of God's love is _____.
   a. Feeling
   b. External attraction
   c. Self-giving
   d. Faithfulness

2. Before God created the world there was nothing outside Himself; therefore, He could only truly love after He created.
   a. True
   b. False

3. Dr. Lawson states that _____ is the highest form of love that there is.
   a. *Eros*
   b. *Agapē*
   c. *Phileia*
   d. *Alētheia*

4. Since God does not change, His love should not be viewed as passionate.
   a. True
   b. False

BIBLE STUDY AND DISCUSSION QUESTIONS

1. Reflect on God's self-giving love. How can you model this love in your relationships with others?
2. Many people conceive of love primarily as a feeling. Is this appropriate in light of the biblical view of God's love?
3. Are there other religious or cultural groups that you sometimes fail to treat lovingly, either implicitly or explicitly? How can reflection on God's love for the lost challenge you? Are there specific passages of Scripture that come to mind?
4. Some people envisage love as accepting another as they are, not requiring them to change. Do you think God treats individuals in this sort of way?

c

How can I have a more God-glorifying marriage.

15

The Foreknowledge of God

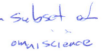
– subset of omniscience

MESSAGE INTRODUCTION

Foreknowledge is an often misunderstood and maligned concept. But many assumptions about its meaning are unbiblical. In this lesson, Dr. Lawson disabuses false notions of foreknowledge and examines what the text of Scripture actually teaches.

SCRIPTURE READINGS

Romans 8:29–30; Acts 2:22–24

TEACHING OBJECTIVES

1. To correct unbiblical views of foreknowledge
2. To explain key passages of Scripture that together provide a clear and coherent picture of God's foreknowledge
3. To inspire trust and confidence in the One who foreknows His people

QUOTATIONS

God knows both the micro- and macro-dimensions of the entire universe. He numbers the very hairs of our heads. Not only does He know what we will do before we do it, but also He knows all the options we could have chosen at the moment. He knows all contingencies. Yet God's knowledge of contingencies is not itself contingent. His foreknowledge is perfect and absolute. He is not a Great Chess Player who must wait to see what we will do, but He knows absolutely what we will do before we do it. Before a word is even formed on our lips, He knows it altogether.

—R.C. Sproul

When we attribute foreknowledge to God, we mean that all things always were, and perpetually remain, under his eyes, so that to his knowledge there is nothing future or past, but all things are present. And they are present in such a way that he not only conceives them through ideas . . . but he truly looks upon them and discerns them as things placed before him.

—John Calvin

LECTURE OUTLINE

A. Correcting Misunderstandings of Foreknowledge
   1. God has never looked into the future and learned anything.
      a. God is omniscient.
      b. He never looks into the future and sees anything He has not already foreordained.
   2. If all God does is look into the future to see what someone will do, then that's all that foreknowledge is.
      a. Since mankind is totally depraved, no one would repent if foreknowledge only entailed observation and not God acting to bring about a state of affairs.
   3. *Foreknowledge* does not mean foresight.
      a. Romans 8:29 states, "*whom* He foreknew," not "*what* He foresaw."
      b. It is a gross misunderstanding of what the word *foreknowledge* means.
      c. *Foreknowledge* more accurately refers to God's previous choice to love a certain group of people.

B. The Biblical Meaning of Foreknowledge
   1. We must first establish the meaning of *know* in Scripture.
      a. Genesis 4:1 says, "Adam knew Eve his wife, and she conceived."
         i. This passage makes it clear that the word *know* in Scripture can mean a loving and intimate relationship. It doesn't always simply mean the knowledge of facts.
      b. Amos 3:2 says, "You only have I known of all the families of the earth."
         i. Here God is speaking of Israel. *Know* here means choosing to love in a very distinguishing way.
      c. Matthew 1:25 says, "[Joseph] knew her not until she had given birth."
         i. This refers again to the intimate relationship between a husband and wife.
      d. Jesus says in Matthew 7:23, "I never knew you."
         i. God knows everything; clearly, He means here that they never had a relationship.
      e. Jesus says in John 10:14, "I know my own and my own know me."
         i. Jesus is speaking here of an intimate, personal, saving relationship.
   2. There are explicit examples of foreknowledge.
      a. Acts 2:23 says Jesus was "delivered up according to the . . . foreknowledge of God."
      b. 1 Peter 1:1–2 says Christians are "elect exiles . . . according to the foreknowledge of God the Father."

15—The Foreknowledge of God 55

        i. Here those who were chosen by the Father were chosen because of the distinguishing love that the Father has for the elect.
- c. Romans 8:29 says, "For those whom he foreknew he also predestined."
    - i. Here we have clear evidence that those who are predestined are those whom the Father has loved in eternity past with a distinguishing affection.

STUDY QUESTIONS

1. When Christ speaks of telling certain individuals that He never knew them, He means _____.
    - a. He didn't condone their behavior
    - b. He had never seen them before
    - c. He did not know where they came from
    - d. He didn't have an intimate relationship with them

2. Foreknowledge consists of God's looking down the tunnel of time to see how men will respond to His Son.
    - a. True
    - b. False

3. Choose the incorrect statement:
    - a. Foreknowledge connotes a relationship and excludes knowledge.
    - b. Foreknowledge is closely related to foreordination.
    - c. Foreknowledge cannot change.
    - d. Foreknowledge was operative before the world began.

4. Foreknowledge is very similar in meaning to foresight.
    - a. True
    - b. False

BIBLE STUDY AND DISCUSSION QUESTIONS

1. Since God's foreknowledge is perfect and doesn't change, what motivation do Christians have for evangelism?

2. Many people struggle with the idea that God foreknows certain individuals but not others. How can you show them that God's foreknowledge actually magnifies His character rather than diminishes His fairness and grace?

3. How can God's eternal foreknowledge encourage believers in times of sorrow?

4. Have you known other Christians who don't adhere to the definition of foreknowledge presented in this lesson? Do they witness to unbelievers differently? Do they talk about the love of God differently?

16

The Wrath of God — action

- Movie: The American Gospel (3) on Netflix
- Ray Comfort

MESSAGE INTRODUCTION

While many people prefer not to think about the wrath of God, the Bible does not hesitate to speak of it. In Scripture, God's wrath serves as a warning to unbelievers and a reason for holy living for His people. In this message, Dr. Lawson looks at the nature and necessity of God's wrath, and the many different ways that it is shown in Scripture.

SCRIPTURE READINGS

Proverbs 1:24–31; Romans 1:18–32

TEACHING OBJECTIVES

1. To explain the necessity and various modes of God's wrath
2. To instill a holy fear in the God who will judge the world
3. To elicit thanksgiving by reflecting on that from which believers are saved, and what it is that Christ suffered

QUOTATIONS

There is the dreadful pit of the glowing flames of the wrath of God; there is hell's wide gaping mouth open; and you have nothing to stand upon, nor any thing to take hold of; there is nothing between you and hell but the air; it is only the power and mere pleasure of God that holds you up.

—Jonathan Edwards

The wisdom of God devised a way for the love of God to deliver sinners from the wrath of God while not compromising the righteousness of God.

—John Piper

16—The Wrath of God

LECTURE OUTLINE

A. The Need for God's Wrath
1. The wrath of God is an expression of His holiness.
2. God cannot be neutral toward sin.

B. The Nature of God's Wrath
1. One aspect of God's wrath is that it is abiding.
    a. God's wrath is already abiding on the heads of sinners (Rom. 1:18).
    b. Right now His mercy is holding it back.
2. It is also catastrophic wrath.
    a. There are individual times in human history when God brings severe judgment upon the human race.
        i. The flood of Genesis 6 and 7.
        ii. The fire and brimstone from heaven on Sodom and Gomorrah.
        iii. The plagues upon the Egyptians.
    b. These are expressions of God's wrath.
3. It is consequential wrath.
    a. God's wrath is revealed in the principle of sowing and reaping (Gal. 6:7; Hos. 8:7).
    b. Sinful actions will be met with God's wrath.
4. It is abandoning wrath.
    a. God's wrath expresses itself when the sinner, after repeatedly rejecting the knowledge of God and the gospel of Christ, is abandoned by God and turned over to the pursuit of their own sins (Rom. 1:24–26).
5. It is eschatological wrath.
    a. This refers to the wrath surrounding the final hour of human history immediately preceding the return of God's Son (Rev. 19).
6. It is eternal wrath.
    a. The wrath of God is displayed in hell (Rev. 20:14).
7. It is redemptive wrath.
    a. This is displayed as Jesus bore believers' sins and suffered on the cross, enduring the wrath of God so that they would never be subject to condemnation.
    b. Every soul will either be damned in hell or will be pardoned in Christ.

STUDY QUESTIONS

1. When God allows individuals to continue in their sin, it is an example of _____.
    a. Abiding wrath
    b. Abandoning wrath
    c. Consequential wrath
    d. None of the above

2. Only those who have knowingly rejected the gospel of Christ will face eternal punishment.
   a. True
   b. False

3. God's wrath is necessitated primarily by His _____.
   a. Omniscience
   b. Goodness
   c. Holiness
   d. Sovereignty

4. Hell is not everlasting.
   a. True
   b. False

BIBLE STUDY AND DISCUSSION QUESTIONS

1. Many people claim that it would be unfair for God to release His wrath on His own creation. How would you respond?
2. People often understand God's wrath in terms of human anger. What are the similarities and differences between the two?
3. Since Christians need no longer stand under the wrath of God, what is the benefit of meditating on this attribute of God?
4. In addition to God's wrath, what other attribute or attributes of God do you see clearly displayed in Christ's crucifixion?

- It puts the other attributes in perspective
- It creates gratitude

- You deserve wrath, and God's grace is a free gift, and we should have gratitude
- We obey out of gratitude for what God has done for us